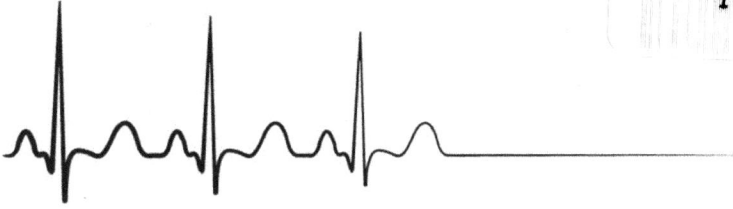

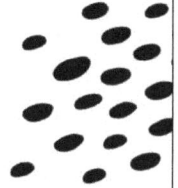

UNDERSTANDING LIFE and DEATH

What Will Happen When I Die?

Janine McNally

ISBN - Paperback: 979-8-9896732-9-2
Second Edition: December 2025.
Printed in the United States of America.

Janine McNally, Th. M., D. Min.
Panama City, FL 32401
Janine@EquippingFireflies.com

Dear Parents

Dear Parent,

In this age of technology and 24/7 news, protecting our children from a world full of tragedy and grief is impossible.

It is essential to prepare them to cope with the scenarios that they will inevitably face by talking with them about death and trauma.

If your family has lost a friend or a relative, your children may have many questions.

- They might not know how to ask the questions.
- You might not know how to answer them.

It's important to address your feelings of grief and distress first and then support your children as they do the same.

The amount of information, details, and language used when addressing their questions will vary with each child, depending on their age and the situation.

UNDERSTANDING LIFE AND DEATH

As they process their grief, you can:

1. Be there for them.
Make sure you are the one who tells them the bad news rather than waiting and having them hear it from someone else. Be available. Spend extra time with them.

2. Give them permission to talk about their thoughts or emotions.
Allow your child time to process what happened and to ask questions. Be honest with them, but don't give them more information than necessary.

3. Don't be afraid to let them see your grief.
It's okay for them to see you cry. It's good for them to see that grief is not over in an instant but takes time to work through.

4. Use simple, concrete language.
Talk to your kids using clear, direct language. Avoid euphemisms and metaphors such as "passed away" or "gone to sleep." They only add confusion to children who are unable to understand abstract language.

5. Reassure them that they are safe and cared for.

In the case of a crime causing the death, reassure them that safeguards have been taken to protect them and to prevent this kind of thing from happening to them.

Let them know that you will be there, no matter what.

6. Talk about heaven.

Give them a glimpse of heaven. The promise of heaven gives hope.

> *"… Weeping may stay for the night, but* ***rejoicing comes in the morning.****"*
> Psalm 30:5 (NIV).

There will be sorrow, but our eternal perspective gives hope.

This book answers many of the common questions that will, no doubt, run through the minds of kids as they think about life and death.

Questions are answered from a Biblical perspective in an age-appropriate way to provide help and hope in a time of sadness and grief.

> *"... do not grieve like the rest of mankind,*
> *who have no hope."*
> 1 Thessalonians 4:13 (NIV).

We are praying for you!
Equipping Fireflies, Inc.

Table of Contents

Questions about Death & Dying 17

1. What is Death?

2. Is Death Forever?

3. Why Do People Get Sick and Die?

4. Does Death Hurt?

5. Why Can't Doctors and Hospitals Stop Someone from Dying?

6. What Happens After You Die?

7. When Someone Dies, Are They Being Punished?

8. If God Loves Me, Why Did My Dad Die?

9. What Happens During a Funeral?

10. Why Do I Feel So Sad?

11. Why Do Some People Die When They Are Young?

12. Was It My Fault?

13. When Will I Die?

14. Will I Die Now, too?

Questions about Heaven 45

1. What is Heaven Like?

2. What Do People Do in Heaven?

3. Will My Pet Be in Heaven?

4. Will We Recognize People in Heaven?

5. Will Everyone Go to Heaven No Matter What They Believe?

6. Is My Grandma in Heaven?

7. If Someone Kills Themself, Will They Go to Heaven

8. Do People Who Never Hear About Jesus Go to Heaven?

9. What About "Good" People?

10. What About Babies Who Die?

Questions about Hell 77

1. Is Hell Real?

2. What is Hell Like?

3. Why Does Hell Last Forever?

4. How Could a Loving God Send People to Hell?

5. Why Didn't God Just Create Perfect People?

6. How Can People Enjoy Heaven Knowing That Others Are Suffering in Hell?

Other Questions...91

1. Are There Really Angels?

2. Who Is Satan?

3. Why Did God Create Satan?

4. Did God Create Other Universes or Just This One?

Congratulations 105

Note to Parents 107

Choosing The Best Bible for Your Child 109

The Understanding Life Series 115

About the Author 123

About the Ministry 125

UNDERSTANDING LIFE AND DEATH

Understanding Life & Death

What Happens When We Die?

UNDERSTANDING LIFE AND DEATH

Introduction

Hey there,
I'm so glad that you are reading this book.

If someone you know and love died, you are no doubt struggling with many different feelings and questions. Hopefully, this book will help a little.

I'm going to be honest with you.

Dealing with someone's death is never easy. Talking about it is sometimes even harder.

- Perhaps you think their death might have been your fault.

- Perhaps you feel guilty about something you did or said.

- Perhaps you are afraid that you will die, too.

It's in times like these that we have lots of questions, like…

- Where is God?

- Why did He let this happen?

- Does He care?

UNDERSTANDING LIFE AND DEATH

I want you to know that God is always with you.
He promises to comfort you and support you through these difficult times.

The Bible says that God will comfort people who are sad.

> *"Blessed are those who are sad. **They will be comforted.**"*
> Matthew 5:4 (NIRV).

It says that God counts every tear that you cry.

> *"List my tears on Your scroll. Are they not **in Your record?**"*
> Psalm 56:8 (NIV).

Jesus knows what it feels like to lose a friend.
Lazarus, His close friend, died.
When He heard the news, Jesus cried and felt pain and sadness.

It's never easy when someone you love dies.

I'm not going to tell you not to worry or be sad.

- It's normal to feel sadness.
- It's normal to cry (and it's OK if you don't).

WHAT HAPPENS WHEN WE DIE?

- It's normal to miss them!

Your feelings might be all over the place. Grief can look like a lot of different things.

- You might feel OK one day and horrible the next.
- You might feel like being alone.
- You might feel guilt or anger.
- You might feel like you need to be brave.
- You might have trouble sleeping.
- You might have difficulty concentrating at school.

You probably feel a LOT of things.
You probably have a LOT of questions!

We all feel differently, and that's OK!

This little book will hopefully answer some of your questions. If you need help reading it, ask a friend or a family member to help you.

You might also want to talk to someone about how you feel. Don't be afraid to tell someone you trust that you need help.

UNDERSTANDING LIFE AND DEATH

Questions About Death & Dying

UNDERSTANDING LIFE AND DEATH

1. What is Death?

Death is a part of life that we don't like to talk about. But death comes to everything that lives.

When Adam sinned in the Garden of Eden by disobeying God's command, one of the consequences was death.

- Plants now die in winter.

- Trees die when they get old or sick.

- Animals die.

- People die, too.

That is how nature works. Where there is life, there is death.

When someone dies, their body stops working.

- They no longer breathe, move, eat, or drink.

- Their heart stops beating.

- They can't feel anything, so they're not in any pain.

- They can't come back to life once they're dead.

The Bible talks a lot about death.

UNDERSTANDING LIFE AND DEATH

We don't like to talk about "death," so people sometimes use other words, like "passed" or "passed away."

Some people say that dying is like falling asleep.
That's true in one sense.

The Bible says that if you love Jesus, you fall asleep and wake up in heaven.

> *"We believe that God will bring with Jesus those who have **fallen asleep** in Him."*
> 1 Thessalonians 4:14 (NIV).

That might make you afraid of falling asleep.
But dying is not the same as **physical** sleep, so there is no need to be afraid of going to sleep. It's completely different from dying.

Some people might tell you that dying is like "going away."

You might be told that Grandma has "gone away."
That's also kind of true. If Grandma had trusted in Jesus, she has "gone away" to heaven.

"Going home" might be a better way of saying it.
Death is a very difficult part of life, but it's something we all experience. If you have questions, keep reading.

2. Is Death Forever?

Yes, death is forever.

When someone dies, nothing can bring them back to life. Their life on earth is over.

You might be thinking, "What about Lazarus?" Lazarus was raised back to life.

Yes, sometimes people are raised back to life by God, but they eventually die (again).

But dying is not the same as going away for a vacation. Once you die, you can't come back.

It's also completely different from dying.

So, to answer the question… Yes, death is forever.

The good news is that if you have trusted in Jesus to save you, you will see your friend or family member again one day!

3. Why Do People Get Sick and Die?

People get sick and die because of the sin that came into the world. When Adam and Eve sinned, death was a consequence.

God never wanted sickness and death.
When God created the world, everything in it was perfect.

Read this verse.

> *"God saw that it was **good**"*
> Genesis 1:10 (NIV).

And when God says that something is "good," it means that it is perfect.

There was no sickness or death.
Everything was good.

So, what went wrong?

When Adam and Eve chose to disobey God in the Garden of Eden, they were guilty of sin.

The Bible tells us that:

> *"**Sin entered the world** because one man sinned.
> And death came because of sin. Everyone sinned,
> **so death came to all people.**"*
> Romans 5:12 (NIRV).

Death is a result of sin, and since we're all sinners, we will all die.

Ever since that day in the Garden of Eden, we have to live with the effects of sin entering into God's perfect creation. Ever since, things have died.

There are many reasons why people get sick and die.

Death can come through accidents, sickness, or old age.

- Sometimes, they are in a bad accident.
- Sometimes, people make bad choices, and those choices have big consequences.
- Sometimes, they have had a serious illness or disease that doctors can't make better.
- Other times, they just get old and die.

We will all die one day. Our physical lives will end.

UNDERSTANDING LIFE AND DEATH

We must be ready because we never know what
tomorrow might bring.

- Kids often think that they are invincible.
- Kids often think that they have a long time to live.

And most of the time, that is true.

But tomorrow is not promised to us.
We need to be ready.

The best news is that if we have trusted in Jesus to save
us, we will go immediately to heaven when we die.

Death is not the end.
If we have trusted in Jesus, death is not something to fear.

4. Does Death Hurt?

People often worry about how painful it will be when they die.

The good news is that doctors tell us that death is not usually painful.

Especially with old people, dying is almost always quiet.

With all of the medicine available now, most people do not have any pain at the end of their life.

When someone dies in a bad accident, they often feel no pain at all because death happens so quickly.

Even when someone is sick or hurt for a long time, doctors have special medicines and treatments that can take away a lot of the pain.

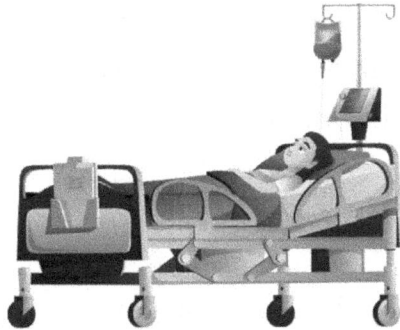

So, no!
Death does not usually hurt.
Phew! That's great news!

5. Why Can't Doctors Stop People from Dying?

Many times, doctors can stop someone from dying. We have amazing hospitals and medicine now.

- Doctors and nurses work hard to make sick and hurt people get better.

- Doctors usually help people live long, healthy lives.

People now live much longer than they did years ago.

Yet sometimes, even with all of our medical knowledge and even though they do their best, the person still dies.

Doctors can only do so much. They are only human.

We will all die one day.

6. When Someone Dies, are they Being Punished?

Why do people die? Are they being punished?

When someone dies, it is almost always natural.

Time wears out important parts of our bodies, and these parts cannot work anymore. People die when parts like the heart, for example, stop working.

God has given us wonderfully strong bodies that usually last a long time, but sickness sometimes makes the body stop working before a person gets old.

Remember:
When sin entered the world, so did death. Death is a result of sin.

That doesn't mean that we are being punished.

Death is just the natural end for humans. Our bodies were only designed to live for a time.

7. If God Loves Me, Why Did My Dad Die?

If God loves me, why did my dad (or someone else) die?

This is a question that we don't know the answer to.

The Bible tells us that everything happens for a reason. There is a bigger plan that only God knows about.

There are many reasons why people die.

And we would all like to know why.

- Why did someone I love have to die?

- Why couldn't it have been someone else?

Death never seems fair.

- Almost everyone is loved by someone.

- Almost everyone will be missed by someone.

We will all lose someone we love someday.

But you are no doubt wondering why God didn't answer your prayers for your dad (or someone else you love) to get better.

WHAT HAPPENS WHEN WE DIE?

The Bible tells us that God loves us and always hears our prayers.

Sometimes, when we pray, God says, "Yes."
But, sometimes, He says, "No."

When God says, "No," He has a reason, and we might never understand.

Just know, if your dad loved Jesus, then he DID get better.

- He is not sick or hurting anymore because he is with Jesus in heaven.
- He has no pain, no suffering, no tears.
- He is happier than you could imagine.

God DID answer your prayers, just not how you hoped.

For Christians, death is like a doorway to heaven.

Imagine, for a minute, where your dad is.

If you really understood what heaven is like, you would be so glad he was there.

UNDERSTANDING LIFE AND DEATH

You wouldn't want him to come back to a life of pain and suffering.

And he wouldn't want to come back.

And even though you won't see your dad for a while, you can trust that God knows best.

God controls every breath we take.
And we know that one day, we will see those we love again.

We have the hope of heaven.

> "… **do not grieve** like the rest of mankind, who have no hope."
> 1 Thessalonians 4:13 (NIV).

8. What Happens After You Die?

People are made up of three parts: their body, soul, and spirit.

Read this verse and fill in the blanks below.

> *"May your whole **spirit**, **soul**, and **body**
> be kept free from blame."*
> 1 Thessalonians 5:23 (NIRV).

People have a S __ __ __ __ __, a S __ __ __ and a

B __ __ __.

Our **soul** is our mind, our emotions, and our will. It is the part of us that lets us feel love and happiness.

Our **spirit** is how we connect with God.

The soul or spirit is not a part of our physical body. We cannot see a person's spirit and soul.

After we die,

- Our physical body, which doesn't work anymore, will be buried.

UNDERSTANDING LIFE AND DEATH

- Our soul and spirit are the part of a person that lives forever.

When a person who loves Jesus dies, their soul and spirit go immediately to be with Jesus in heaven.

9. What Happens During a Funeral?

A funeral is a ceremony where we say "goodbye" to someone we love and celebrate their life.

When our pet dies, we often bury them in the backyard. When people die, we usually bury them in the cemetery.

Usually, in America, family and friends gather for a funeral to remember the person who died.

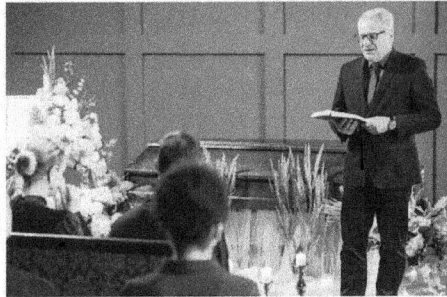

It's a time to say "goodbye," and show their love (both for the person and their family and friends).

During the funeral service:

- People usually tell stories about the person who died. They will laugh and cry as they remember the good times they shared.

- There are often photos of the person around the room to help you remember all the special times.

- There might be prayers and singing.

UNDERSTANDING LIFE AND DEATH

All of these are ways to remember that person and celebrate their life.

Funerals usually happen a few days after the person dies. They are usually held at a Funeral Home.

- Sometimes, the coffin is there.

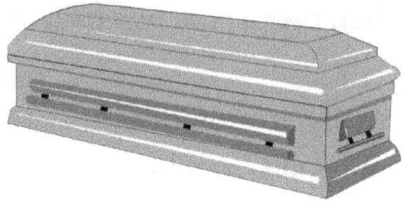

- Sometimes, the coffin is open, and you can see the body of the person who died.

After the funeral, close family and friends will travel by car to the cemetery for a graveside service.

- A small tent and chairs will be set up for the family to sit.

- There is usually a short service by the pastor.

- People will often place a flower on the coffin.

After everyone leaves, the coffin will be lowered into the
ground and buried.

Sometime later, a
headstone will be placed
to mark the grave.

Sometimes, instead of a funeral, people will have a
Memorial Service.

Memorial Services often happen a few weeks later when
some of the family members live far away and need time
to organize their trip.

Since some time has passed, people are often ready to
remember the happy times. There are fewer tears and
more good memories.

10. Why Do I Feel So Sad?

It's normal to have lots of feelings when someone dies. You've just lost someone that you loved.

What you are feeling is called 'grief.' Grief is when we feel sad about our loss.

Grief can look really different for each person.

You might feel fear, anger, confusion, or sadness. We all struggle with grief.

Just remember:

- It's ok to cry.
- It's ok to ask, "Why?"

Grief can come and go, and sometimes lasts a long time.

Sad feelings don't last forever.

They will probably come and go, and as time passes, you will be able to celebrate the good memories and be happy again.

WHAT HAPPENS WHEN WE DIE?

If someone you love has died, you might feel like it's wrong to be happy again.

But they would want you to be happy.

- It's OK to laugh and play.
- It's OK to move on.

Maybe you could find a way to celebrate their memory each year on the anniversary of their death.

You could make a card or pick a flower and take it to the cemetery.

No doubt some things will change for you and your family. Things might be different from what they were.

You will never forget them, but being happy and having fun is OK. That's what they would want.

No matter what you feel, it's ok.

Don't be afraid to ask questions and share how you feel with people you love and trust.

11. Why Do Some People Die When They Are Young?

Most people are strong and healthy and will live until they are very old.

The Bible tells us that a normal life is seventy years, or eighty if we are very strong.

> "Our days may come to **seventy years or eighty** if our strength endures."
> Psalm 90:10 (NIV).

But sometimes, people die when they are young. Sometimes, they get sick, or they might be in an accident.

A young person's death is especially sad.

It doesn't feel fair. It seems like everyone should live a long, happy life.

But, unfortunately, that's not the way things always work.

Sometimes, people die when they are young.

12. Was it My Fault?

You might wonder, "Was it my fault that they died?"

NO! Absolutely not!

- Maybe you argued with them.
- Maybe you even fought with them.
- So, now you feel really guilty.

Being naughty or mean doesn't make someone die.
And being kind doesn't stop someone from dying, either.

- It is not their fault.
- It is not your fault.
- It is not God's fault.

Nothing that you said or did caused this to happen.

Everyone says and does things that later they wish they hadn't. But that doesn't make someone die.

Remember: You are not to blame! There's nothing that you could have done to stop the person from dying.

Death is a part of life.
And if we have trusted in Jesus to save us, it's the doorway to eternal life in heaven.

13. When Will I Die?

Many people wonder about when they will die.

Unfortunately, we won't know

It might be today, next week, or next year. Or maybe in fifty years.

Eventually, everyone dies.
All living things die.

Trees, flowers, animals,
and, yes, even people.

Every living thing has a lifetime, a beginning, and an end.

Flowers begin bright and beautiful. A few days after they are picked, they begin to droop and wilt.

And then they die.

We will all die one day.
Coffins come in all sizes.

Usually, children are healthy and strong and live a long time.

WHAT HAPPENS WHEN WE DIE?

Usually, children don't die until they're much older.

We don't know how many days we will have on this earth, but God does.

The Bible tells us that every day is measured.
God has numbered our days, from before we were even born until the day we die.

Read this verse.

> *"All the days ordained for me **were written in Your book** before one of them came to be."*
> Psalm 139:16 (NIV).

God has written all of the days of our lives in His
B __ __ __.

The writer of this next verse wanted to know when He would die.

> *"Show me, Lord, my life's end and the number of my days."*
> Psalm 39:4 (NIV).

But only God knows how many days we will live.

Read this verse.

> *"A person's days are determined;*
> **You have decreed the number of his months**
> *and have set limits he cannot exceed."*
> Job 14:5 (NIV).

Our days are D __ __ __ __ __ __ __ __ __.

That's a big word that means our days are already numbered. God has planned out our days.

Nothing we do will change that.

Only God knows how long we will live.

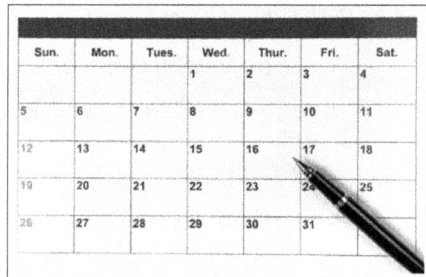

Sun.	Mon.	Tues.	Wed.	Thur.	Fri.	Sat.
			1	2	3	4
5	6	7	8	9	10	11
12	13	14	15	16	17	18
19	20	21	22	23	24	25
26	27	28	29	30	31	

Remember:
God has written all the days of our lives in His book. So, there is no need to be afraid.

Read these verses.

> **"In His hand is the life** *of every creature*
> *and the breath of all mankind."*
> Job 12:10 (NIV).

WHAT HAPPENS WHEN WE DIE?

> *"My times are in Your hands."*
> Psalm 31:15 (NIV).

There is no need to fear.
Our lives are in God's H __ __ __ __.

Believe it or not, as you get older and your body begins to wear out, the idea of a brand-new body with no pain and suffering begins to sound good.

Older people begin to look forward to heaven and being with Jesus.

Any fear of death is gone!
In fact, death is something to look forward to.

Heaven is waiting for us.

UNDERSTANDING LIFE AND DEATH

Questions About Heaven

UNDERSTANDING LIFE AND DEATH

1. What is Heaven Like?

The Bible tells us quite a few things about heaven.

Read these Bible verses and fill in the blanks.

> *"Then I looked and heard the **voice of many angels**, numbering thousands upon thousands, and ten thousand times ten thousand."*
> Revelation 5:11 (NIV).

Heaven is full of singing A __ __ __ __ __.

> *"Also, in front of the throne, there was what looked like **a sea** of glass, clear as crystal."*
> Revelation 4:6 (NIV).

There is a S __ __.

> *"Then the angel showed me **the river of the water of life**, as clear as crystal,
> flowing from the throne of God and of the Lamb."*
> Revelation 22:1 (NIV).

And a R __ __ __ __.

> *"The glow of an emerald circled His **throne** like a rainbow."*
> Revelation 4:3 (NIV).

And a T __ __ __ __ __.

> *"And he carried me away in the Spirit to a **mountain**
> great and high, and showed me the Holy **City**, Jerusalem,
> coming down out of heaven from God. It shone with the
> glory of God, and its brilliance was like that of a very
> precious jewel, like a jasper, clear as crystal."*
> Revelation 21:10-11 (NIV).

And a M __ __ __ __ __ __ __ and a C __ __ __.

> *"It had a great, high **wall** with **twelve**
> gates and with twelve angels at the gates."*
> Revelation 21:12 (NIV).

And a W __ __ __ with twelve gates.

The light of God's love is always shining in heaven.

> *"Its gates will never be shut
> because there will be **no night there**."*
> Revelation 21:25 (NIRV).

Heaven has no N __ __ __ __.

> *"There will be no more night. They **will not need the light of a lamp or the light of the sun,** for the Lord God will give them light. And they will reign for ever and ever."*
> Revelation 22:5 (NIV).

There will be no need for L __ __ __ __ or the S __ __.

> *"My Father's house has **many rooms**...*
> *I am going there to prepare a place for you."*
> John 14:2 (NIV).

There will be many R __ __ __ __.

The Bible tells us that the streets will be made of gold, and fine jewels will be crafted in the foundation.

Best of all, Jesus is there.
He is taking care of the people we love who have gone to be with Him in Heaven.

2. What Do People Do in Heaven?

Do you ever wonder what we will do in heaven?
We're not told much, but here are a few things.

1. We will eat and drink.

The Bible tells us that there will be food.

I'm guessing it will be like a five-star restaurant, unlike anything here on earth.

Read these verses and fill in the blanks below.

> *"And while they still did not believe it because of joy and amazement, He asked them, "Do you have anything here to eat?" They gave Him a piece of broiled fish, and He took it and **ate it** in their presence."*
> Luke 24:41-43 (NIV).

When Jesus rose from the dead, He was in His new resurrected body.

Even though He no longer needed food to live, we know that He still ate.

The disciples gave Jesus a piece of F __ __ __.

> *"… you may **eat and drink** at my table in My kingdom and sit on thrones, judging the twelve tribes of Israel."*
> Luke 22:30 (NIV).

We will E __ __ and D __ __ __ __ in God's kingdom.

> *"On each side of the river grew a tree of life, bearing **twelve crops of fruit, with a fresh crop each month."***
> Revelation 22:2 (NIV).

The trees will provide F __ __ __ __ every month.

> *"**Never again will they hunger;** never again will they **thirst.**"*
> Revelation 7:16 (NIV).

There will be no H __ __ __ __ __ or T __ __ __ __.

We won't need to eat or drink, so it will just be for fun.

Imagine how good it will be.

2. We will be celebrating with many people.

You will never be lonely.

> *"After this, I looked, and there before me was a great multitude that no one could count,*
> *from **every nation, tribe, people, and language**,*
> *standing before the throne and before the Lamb."*
> Revelation 7:9 (NIV).

There will be people from every nation, tribe, people, and language.

That's a LOT of people!
We will spend eternity getting to know them all.

3. We will run, walk, dance, and sing.

> *"And you will **sing** as on the night you **celebrate** a holy festival; your hearts will **rejoice** as when people playing pipes go up."*
> Isaiah 30:29 (NIV).

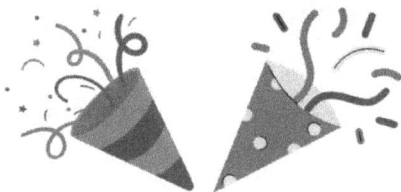

4. We will worship and serve God.

> "The throne of God and of the Lamb will be in the city, and His servants **will serve Him.**"
> Revelation 22:3 (NIV).

We are not told everything about heaven.

God is hiding heaven's treasures.

> "In whom are hidden **all the treasures** of wisdom and knowledge."
> Colossians 2:3 (NIV).

It will be like one BIG surprise party.

It will be wonderful beyond our wildest imagination!

- Imagine the best life ever.

- Imagine being so happy all the time that you feel like you will burst.

- Imagine all of the good things you have here and none of the bad.

Then multiply that by a hundred, and you're getting close to what it will be like in heaven.

3. Will My Pet Be in Heaven?

We all wonder about our
"best friends."

What will happen to them?

The Bible tells us that God
cares about animals.

Read these Bible verses.

> "The righteous **care for the
> needs of their animals**."
> Proverbs 12:10 (NIV).

God created animals, so we know that He values them.

> "God made the **wild anim**als according to their kinds, the
> **livestock** according to their kinds, and all the **creatures**
> that move along the ground according to their kinds.
> And God saw that it was good."
> Genesis 1:25 (NIV).

He made almost endless varieties, colors, and species.

He saved them during the flood.

> *"Pairs of all creatures that have the breath of life in them came to Noah **and entered the ark.**"*
> Genesis 7:15 (NIV).

Two of every kind of animal entered the A __ __ with Noah.

> *"In His hand is the **life of every creature** and the breath of all mankind."*
> Job 12:10 (NIV).

He holds the life of EVERY creature in His H __ __ __.

We know that there are animals in God's kingdom.

> *"I saw heaven standing open and there before me was a **white horse.**"*
> Revelation 19:11 (NIV).

There is a white H __ __ __ __.

> *"The **wolf** will live with the **lamb**, the **leopard** will lie down with the **goat**, the **calf** and the **lion** and the **yearling** together, and a little child will lead them. The **cow** will feed with the **bear**, their young will lie down together, and the **lion** will eat straw like the **ox**."*
> Isaiah 11:6-7 (NIV).

There are wolves, lambs, leopards, goats, calves, lions, cows, and bears.

> *"Then I heard **every creature** in heaven and on earth and under the earth and on the sea, and all that is in them, saying, "To Him who sits on the throne and to the Lamb be praise and honor and glory and power, for ever and ever!"*
> Revelation 5:13 (NIV).

There will be E __ __ __ __ creature.

So, I can't imagine there won't be dogs, cats, and bunnies too.

> *"You, Lord, preserve both people and **animals**."*
> Psalm 36:6 (NIV).

God cares about them all.

> *"For every **animal** of the forest is Mine, and the **cattle** on a thousand hills. I know every **bird** in the mountains, and the **insects** in the fields are Mine."*
> Psalm 50:10-11 (NIV).

When Jesus comes back to bring us to heaven, He will make everything perfect.

We don't know for sure if our pets will go to heaven, but we do know that God cares about them all.

- He is their Creator.

- He is perfect and good.

- He loves animals.

- He created them for our enjoyment.

It would be easy for Him to bring our pets to heaven. So, we can be sure He has a good plan for us and our pets.

4. Will We Recognize People in Heaven?

The Bible seems to suggest that, yes, we will recognize people in heaven, perhaps even more than we know them now.

> *"Now we see only a dim likeness of things. It is as if we were seeing them in a foggy mirror. But someday, we will see clearly. **We will see face to face.** What I know now is not complete. But someday, I will know completely, just as God knows me completely."*
> 1 Corinthians 13:12 (NIRV).

We will know people more completely, just like God knows them.

But things will be different.
Our appearance will be different because God will give us new bodies, similar to Jesus' resurrection body.

When Jesus came back to life after He died on the cross, His disciples saw His physical body change into His new heavenly body.

> *"There in front of them, **His appearance was changed.** His face shone like the sun. His clothes became as white as the light."*
> Matthew 17:2 (NIRV).

But His disciples still recognized Him.

Our new bodies will be perfect.

- We will never grow old, tired, or die.

- We will never again feel pain.

But yes, we will know each other.

5. Will Everyone Go to Heaven No Matter What They Believe?

There are many religions around the world that are full of people who "believe" many different things.

- Many people believe that if you do good things, you will go to heaven.

- Many think that if you believe hard enough, you will be saved.

- Some even believe that if you kill people from other religions, then you will go to "paradise."

However, "believing" is not what is important.

It's not how hard you believe but who you believe.
Jesus said,

> *"I am the Way and the Truth and the Life.
> No one comes to the Father, **except through Me.**"*
> John 14:6 (NIV).

Believing in "something" isn't enough to get someone to heaven. It has to be the right "thing."

The only way we can be saved is by believing in Jesus.

If someone thinks they can find another way to heaven, they're not listening. There is only ONE God.

> *"You shall have **no other gods before Me.**"*
> Exodus 20:3 (NIV).

God sent His Son, Jesus, to earth to pay the price of sin for anyone who believes in Him.

Read these Bible verses.

> *"Salvation is found in no one else,*
> *for there is no other name under heaven given*
> *to mankind by which we must be saved."*
> Acts 4:12 (NIV).

> *"For God so loved the world that He gave His one*
> *and only Son, that whoever believes in **Him***
> *[Jesus] shall not perish but have eternal life."*
> John 3:16 (NIV).

Only by believing in J __ __ __ __ as our Savior can we know we will be in heaven one day.

6. Is My Grandma in Heaven?

That's a great question.

The good news is that if she believed in Jesus, then YES! She is in heaven with Jesus right now!

- She is no longer in any pain.

- She is no longer sick.

- She is no longer sad.

- She is happier than we could imagine.

- She has a new body and will never again get sick.

> *"We are confident, I say, and would prefer to be away from the body and **at home with the Lord**."*
> 2 Corinthians 5:8 (NIV).

She is at H __ __ __ with the Lord.

But what if you don't know what she believed?

It's hard to imagine that some people will not go to heaven.

But that's what the Bible says.

WHAT HAPPENS WHEN WE DIE?

We cannot know for sure what people believe.

That is between them and God.

- They might say that they believe.

- They might say that they don't believe.

We have to trust that God knows best.

> *"Will not the Judge of all the earth **do right**?"*
> Genesis 18:25 (NIV).

We must trust God's love and justice.

7. If Someone Commits Suicide, Will They Go to Heaven?

When someone ends their own life, it is called "suicide."

There are many reasons why people might do this. Usually, the people who do this are REALLY sad and don't know how to fix it.

It's always difficult because there were other ways to solve their problems.

Instead, the choice was to give up.

- Suicide hurts other people so much.
- Suicide hurts God, too.

But suicide is just a wrong choice, just like other wrong choices.

It's a sin, but it's just like other sins.

It is sad, but if they loved Jesus, they would still go to heaven.

Remember: God forgives ALL of our sins!

8. Do People Who Never Hear About Jesus Go to Heaven?

This is a difficult question that will take a little longer to answer.

Do people who have never heard still go to heaven? Here is what the Bible teaches.

1. Creation

The Bible tells us that everyone has been given enough truth to decide whether to seek God or not – in creation.

All you have to do is look at the tall, snow-covered mountains.

And the powerful ocean waves.

Just watch a beautiful sunset.

Or look carefully at the petals of a flower.

Our amazing world shows that God is our Creator.

> *"Ever since the world was created, it has been possible to see the qualities of God that are not seen. I'm talking about* **His eternal power** *and about the fact that He is God. Those things can be seen in what He has made. So, people have no excuse for what they do."*
> Romans 1:20 (NIRV).

When we look at creation,

- We can see God's qualities – what He is like.

- We can see God's power.

- We can see that He is God.

The Bible says that because of creation, people have no excuse for what they do. Seeing God's power in creation gives them enough information to seek Him.

2. Conscience

God has also given each person a **conscience** to know good and evil.

Everyone has a God-given moral compass.
We were born with an understanding of right and wrong.

Read this verse and fill in the blanks below.

> "They show that what the law requires **is written on their hearts**. The way **their minds judge them** proves this fact. Sometimes, their thoughts find them guilty. At other times, their thoughts find them not guilty."
> Romans 2:15 (NIRV).

God's law (of right and wrong) has been written in our H _ _ _ _ _.

Our minds J _ _ _ _ us.
They tell us what is wrong and right.

Our thoughts sometimes find us G _ _ _ _ _.

Those thoughts are from God.
It is our conscience telling us when we are wrong.

How we respond to our conscience is a choice that we all make.

So, because of **creation** and our **conscience**, we know enough to respond to God.

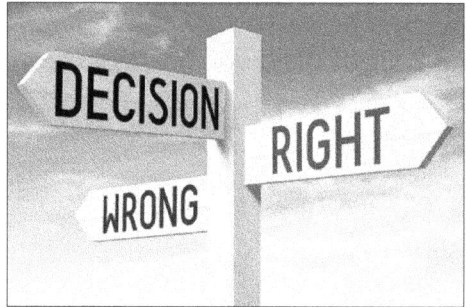

We know enough so that *"people are without excuse."*

That knowledge of God is not enough, however.
We also need to hear about Jesus.

Believing in Jesus is the only way to get to heaven.

So, what happens if people live in a place without churches or Christians?

- If people respond to God when they see **creation**, then God will respond to them.

- If people respond to their **conscience**, then God will find them.

WHAT HAPPENS WHEN WE DIE?

The Bible promises that if we seek God, we will find Him.

God will send someone to them who will tell them about Jesus.

So perhaps the question should be: "What happens to people who turn against God?"

- They have seen creation.

- They know what is right and wrong.

- But they choose to turn against God.

There is always a consequence to the choices that we make.

We might not like the idea of a final judgment.
But we will all be held responsible for our actions.

God is not only love, but He is perfect justice as well.
God hates sin and must punish wrong.

Justice always requires payment for crimes.
It's right that criminals go to prison for their crimes.

The Bible says that we are ALL sinners.

> *"For all have sinned and fall short of the glory of God."*
> Romans 3:23 (NIV).

And sin results in death.

> *"For the wages of sin is death."*
> Romans 6:23.

If God were being "fair," we would ALL go to hell.

To allow sinful humans into God's perfect heaven would mean that heaven was no longer perfect.

That's why the perfect Son of God died on the cross to take our place.

If we refuse Jesus' payment, we must pay the price ourselves.

9. What About "Good" People?

Many people today believe that if they are "good," then they will get into heaven.

"If the good outweighs the bad."

God, however, doesn't agree.
How "good" is "good" enough?
How "bad" is too "bad'?

Who deserves to go to hell?

I'm sure that you would agree that it makes sense for someone like Hitler to be punished.

There should be a judgment, but it should be reserved for the really bad people out there—the terrorists, the murderers, those who abuse children?

That's who belongs in hell, right?

But what about sweet Grandma Mary?
Grandma Mary is the nicest person that you could ever meet.

- She pays her bills on time.
- She bakes cookies for the neighbor's kids.

- She helps with the food pantry in town.

- She even goes to church sometimes.

She's just not into the whole "God" thing.
She thinks that if she's good enough, then she'll be OK.

Does she deserve to go to hell?

The problem with thinking this way is that God's standard for being "good" is 100% perfection.

If we were good 100% of the time, with 0% bad, then we would meet God's standard of perfection.

But NONE of us is that "good."
We are all sinners, guilty of doing wrong.

How does God feel about our "good" works?

Read this verse.

> *"All of us have become like one who is unclean,
> and **all our righteous acts are like filthy rags.**"*
> Isaiah 64:6 (NIV).

God sees all of the good things we do, like F __ __ __ __ __
R __ __ __ .

Compared to God's standard, our works mean nothing.

So, it doesn't matter how many "good" things we do. We will never meet God's standard of perfection.

But because of God's love, He chases after us anyway.

God has shown His love to people in many ways, including Grandma Mary.

- She has seen beautiful sunsets and snow-covered mountain ranges.
- She has seen the mighty ocean waves and the beautiful rose petals.
- She has driven past Christmas nativity scenes and celebrated Easter with a nice meal and an Easter egg hunt.

The problem is that Grandma Mary doesn't think that she needs Jesus.

Each time, she chose to say "no" to God's voice.

- She thinks that she can save herself.
- She doesn't need God.

So, it is not a question of God 'sending us' to hell. People choose to go to hell when they refuse God.

10. What About Babies Who Die?

Babies are too young to understand the good news of
Jesus and believe.

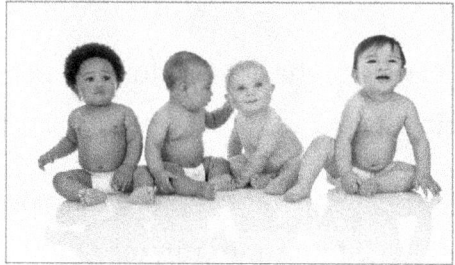

But have you ever seen a
toddler throw a temper
fit?

Babies are sinners and need to be saved, just like everyone
else.

And salvation is only through Jesus.

So, what happens to babies or children who are too young
to understand their need to trust in Jesus?

Or what about people who are mentally disabled and not
capable of understanding?

Most people believe that children go immediately to be
with Jesus when they die.

But what does the Bible say?

WHAT HAPPENS WHEN WE DIE?

The Bible doesn't tell us exactly, but it does teach us what God is like.

1. God is Love.

God loves all children.

> *"It is the same with your Father in heaven.*
> **He does not want any of these little ones to die."**
> Matthew 18:14 (NIRV).

God doesn't want any little children to D __ __.

We can trust our loving God to save those who cannot believe.

2. Jesus loves children.

Read these verses.

> *"People were also bringing babies to Jesus. They wanted Him to place His hands on the babies. When the disciples saw this, they told the people to stop.*
> *But Jesus asked the children to come to Him.*
> **"Let the little children come to Me,"** *He said.*
> **"Don't keep them away."**
> Luke 18:15-16 (NIRV).

Jesus said, "Let the little children C __ __ __ to Me."

UNDERSTANDING LIFE AND DEATH

The God of all love has a plan for children who are too young to believe.

There is a sad story in the Bible about David.
His young son died.

After he died, David said:

> *"But now he's dead. So why should I continue to go without food? Can I bring him back to life again?* **Someday I'll go to him.** *But he won't return to me."*
> 2 Samuel 12:23 (NIRV).

David knew that death was final.
David knew that his son would not return to earth.

But David believed that one day, he would go to him.
One day, David knew he would see his son again in heaven.

When a baby dies, the pain is unimaginable.

But just remember.

God is good, just, and merciful.
God is never unfair.
He would never judge someone who is unable to believe.
We can trust Him to do the right thing!

Questions About Hell

UNDERSTANDING LIFE AND DEATH

1. Is Hell Real?

How could a loving God create a place like hell?
Even worse, how could a loving God send "good" people
to a place like hell?

The Bible talks a lot about hell.

Jesus Taught About Hell.

> *"You nest of poisonous snakes!
> How will you escape from being sentenced **to hell?**"*
> Matthew 23:33 (NIRV).

Jesus told the hypocritical religious leaders that they
would be sentenced to H __ __ __.

Jesus says that those who didn't respond to Him would
go there.

> *"Then they will go away to **eternal punishment,**
> but the righteous to eternal life."*
> Matthew 25:46 (NIRV).

Jesus spoke about hell more than He spoke about heaven.
He spoke about hell more than anyone else in the Bible.

The New Testament Writers Taught About Hell.

Paul declared that those who do not believe the good news about Jesus would go there.

> *"They will be punished with **everlasting destruction** and **shut out from the presence of the Lord** and from the glory of His might."*
> 2 Thessalonians 1:9 (NIV).

Jude said that the people of Sodom and Gomorrah are suffering there.

> *"… an example of those who will suffer the punishment of **eternal fire**."*
> Jude 7 (NIV).

The Bible refers to hell over 162 times in the New Testament alone.

More than 70 are by Jesus.

So, yes.
Hell is a real place.

2. What is Hell Like?

Many of the bible verses that mention "hell" describe what it is like.

Read these verses and fill in the blanks below.

> *"Then they will go away to **eternal punishment,**
> but the righteous to eternal life."*
> Matthew 25:46 (NIRV).

Hell is a place of

E _ _ _ _ _ _ P _ _ _ _ _ _ _ _ _ _.

> *"They will be punished with **everlasting destruction**
> and **shut out from the presence of the Lord** and
> from the glory of His might."*
> 2 Thessalonians 1:9 (NIV).

Hell is a place of

E _ _ _ _ _ _ _ _ _ _ D _ _ _ _ _ _ _ _ _

People will be shut out from God's P _ _ _ _ _ _ _.

Hell is a place of loneliness and separation from God.

> *"But the subjects of the kingdom will be thrown outside into the **darkness**,*
> *where there will be **weeping and gnashing of teeth**."*
> Matthew 8:12 (NIV).

Hell is a place of D __ __ __ __ __ __ __.

There will be W __ __ __ __ __ __ and

G __ __ __ __ __ __ __ of teeth.

Gnashing your teeth means to grind them together when you are angry.

> *"They will be **tormented** with burning sulfur in the presence of the holy angels and of the Lamb.*
> *And the smoke of their **torment** will rise for ever and ever."*
> Revelation 14:10–11 (NIV).

Hell is a place of T __ __ __ __ __ __.

> *"… Where 'the worms that eat them do not die,*
> *and the **fire is not quenched**.'"*
> Mark 9:48 (NIV).

Jesus described it as a place *"where the fire never goes out."*

> *"They will be consigned*
> *to **the fiery lake of burning sulfur**."*
> Revelation 21:8 (NIV).

Hell is a lake of F __ __ __ and burning S __ __ __ __ __.

Sulfur burns like in a volcano.
It smells terrible and causes coughing, shortness of breath, and sore eyes.

This Bible verse uses **"figurative language."** The writers are painting a picture with their words.

But these words are describing a real place.
They are describing a place that no one would want to go.

Imagine a place where there is nothing good.
Imagine your life with everything good taken out.

- No family.

- No friends.

- No love.

- No happiness.

That is what hell will be like.

3. Why Does Hell Last Forever?

You might think…

Everlasting punishment?

- Isn't that a little harsh?
- Don't you think that's a bit cruel?

But why does it have to go on forever?
Wouldn't a thousand years be enough?

The problem is that Hell is full of people who are **not** sorry for what they have done.

Read this Bible verse.

> *"… its kingdom was plunged into darkness. People gnawed their tongues in agony and **cursed the God of heaven** because of their pains and their sores, but **they refused to repent of what they had done**."*
> Revelation 16:10-11 (NIV).

The people in hell will still C __ __ __ __ God.

They still R __ __ __ __ __ to turn from their sins.

In hell, their hearts will become harder.

WHAT HAPPENS WHEN WE DIE?

In heaven, people only choose "good."
In hell, people continue to choose "evil."

Hell goes on forever because sinners never stop sinning.

Remember:

God is the Judge.

He is righteous and just.

He always does what is right.

And He knows what He is doing.

4. How Could a Loving God Send People to Hell?

God didn't create hell for people.

Read this verse.

> "Then He [God] will say to those on His left, 'Depart from He, you who are cursed, into the eternal fire **prepared for the devil and his angels.**"
> Matthew 25:41 (NIV).

Hell was made for the D __ __ __ __ (Satan) and his fallen

A __ __ __ __ __.

It was never intended to be for people.
But man sinned and disobeyed God.

So, God does not "send" anybody anywhere.

We chose to disobey God's perfect plan.

A better question to ask would be:
"Why will some people go to hell?"

We have already learned that we are sinners.

WHAT HAPPENS WHEN WE DIE?

> *"For all have sinned and fall short of the glory of God."*
> Romans 3:23 (NIV).

We know that the penalty for sin is death (Romans 6:23).

> *"For the wages of sin is death."*
> Romans 6:23 (NIV).

We have fallen short of God's perfect standard and must pay the penalty for it.

The penalty is D __ __ __ __.

God is the perfect Judge.

- He doesn't leave things unpunished.

- He cannot forget about justice.

The good news is that even though we all deserve punishment and we all deserve to go to hell, God has provided a way out for us.

God loved us so much that He sent His Son, Jesus, to pay our sin penalty.

Jesus took our place and died on the cross so that we wouldn't have to.

> *"For God so loved the world that **He gave His one and only Son**, that whoever believes in Him shall not perish but have eternal life."*
> John 3:16 (NIV).

God promises that if we believe in Him, we will live forever with Him in heaven.

Do you believe that?

_____

How could a loving God send people to hell?

That's a hard question, for sure.
But a better question we should ask is,

"How could a holy God allow me into His heaven?"

5. Why Didn't God Just Create Perfect People?

Why didn't God just create perfect people so there would be no need for hell?

If God did that, He would have just been creating robots.

He would tell us what to do, and we would do it.
100% perfect obedience.

But if God forced us to obey, that would not be love.
Love is only love when it is voluntary.

God wants our love.
He doesn't want automated robots.

Instead, God gave us a "free will" to choose right from wrong, good from evil.

We can choose to do whatever we want.

Because God honors our choices, He will never force us.

He wants us to choose Him.

6. How Can People Enjoy Heaven Knowing Others Are Suffering in Hell?

Heaven will be filled with people who trust in Jesus for their salvation.

Unfortunately, not everyone will be there.

- The Bible doesn't tell us if we will remember those people.

- We are not told if we will be aware of the people in hell.

But we will not be sad since there are only good things in heaven.

Knowing that our loved ones might end up in hell should cause us to pray hard for them while there is still time.

Other Questions

UNDERSTANDING LIFE AND DEATH

1. Are There Really Angels?

God created angels before He created the world.

Read these Bible verses.

> *"Then I looked and heard the voice of **millions and millions of angels**. They surrounded the throne."*
> Revelation 5:11 (NIRV).

The Bible tells us that there are M __ __ __ __ __ __ __ and

M __ __ __ __ __ __ __ of angels in heaven.

The book of Job describes the angels worshiping God as He was creating the world:

> *"When it happened, the morning stars **sang together**. All the angels **shouted with joy**."*
> Job 38:7 (NIRV).

Angels have other jobs too.

> *"All angels are spirits who serve. God sends them **to serve those who will receive salvation**."*
> Hebrews 1:14 (NIRV).

One of their duties is to S __ __ __ __ people who have trusted in Jesus.

> *"For He [God] will command His angels*
> *concerning you to guard you in all your ways;*
> *they will lift you up in their hands, so that you*
> *will not strike your foot against a stone."*
> Psalm 91:11-12 (NIV).

Angels G _ _ _ _ us.

They L _ _ _ us up.

They protect us.

Another thing angels do is to worship God around His throne.

> *"Then I looked and heard the voice of millions and millions*
> *of angels. They* **surrounded the throne.**
> *They surrounded the living creatures and the elders.*
> *In a loud voice, they were saying,*
> *"The Lamb, who was put to death, is worthy!* **He is**
> **worthy to receive power and wealth and wisdom and**
> **strength!**
> **He is worthy to receive honor and glory and praise!"**
> Revelation 5:11-12 (NIRV).

So, yes, there are angels.

Will you ever meet one?

You just never know!

> *"Do not forget to show hospitality to strangers, for by so doing, **some people have shown hospitality to angels without knowing it.**"*
> Hebrews 13:2 (NIV).

2. Who Is Satan?

When we think of Satan, we sometimes imagine a wicked red creature with horns and a pitchfork.

But that is not what Satan is like.

Satan has many names in the Bible.

He was first known as "Lucifer."
He was the most beautiful angel of all.

But then he became known as "Satan" or the "devil" after he disobeyed God.

Satan is known as the "serpent" who tricked Adam and Eve into disobeying God.

His name means "adversary" or "enemy."
Satan became God's enemy, and he now works to destroy us.

The name "devil" means "accuser."

Satan accuses God's children night and day, trying to get them into trouble.

> *"Satan himself pretends to be an **angel of light**."*
> 2 Corinthians 11:14 (NIRV).

He pretends to be an angel of L __ __ __ __.
He pretends to be good.

Satan wants to trick us into following him.

God created hell for Satan and his angels.
One day, they will be punished forever.

3. Why Did God Create Satan?

God created the angels to serve Him.

Lucifer was God's highest and most beautiful angel.

Read this verse and fill in the blanks below.

> *"You [Satan] were the **model of perfection**. You were **full of wisdom**. You were **perfect and beautiful**."*
> Ezekiel 28:12 (NIRV).

Satan was a model of P __ __ __ __ __ __ __ __ __.

He was full of W __ __ __ __ __.

He was B __ __ __ __ __ __ __ __ __.

Satan was God's highest angel until he chose to turn against God.

> *"Your conduct was without blame from the day you were created. But **soon you began to sin**."*
> Ezekiel 28:12, 15 (NIRV).

He became known as "Satan" when He tried to take God's place.

Satan was not happy with being number two.

- He was full of pride.

- He wanted to be in charge.

- He wanted to be God.

So, God cast Satan out of heaven.

> *"Jesus replied, "I saw **Satan**
> fall like lightning from heaven."*
> Luke 10:18 (NIRV).

> *"You thought you were the bright morning star.
> But now you **have fallen from heaven!**"*
> Isaiah 14:12 (NIRV).

What did Satan do wrong?

Read these verses and draw a circle around the words "I"
and "I'll" in the following verses.

> *"You said in your heart, 'I will go up to the heavens.
> I'll raise my throne above the stars of God.
> I'll sit as king on the mountain where the gods meet.
> I'll set up my throne on the highest slopes of Mount
> Zaphon. I will rise above the tops of the clouds.
> I'll make myself like the Most High God.'"*
> Isaiah 14:13-14 (NIRV).

Six times, Satan said, "I."
Did you find them all?

Satan became proud.
It became all about him.

> "You **thought you were so handsome that it made your heart proud. You thought you were so glorious** that it spoiled your wisdom. So, I threw you down to the earth. I made an example out of you in front of kings."
> Ezekiel 28:16–17 (NIRV).

Sin begins when we say (or think) "I."

- I want to do that.

- I want to be them.

- I want to go there.

We put ourselves first. Number 1.

Did God create "Satan?"

No.
He created a beautiful angel with a free choice.

And Satan chose to turn away from God.

4. Did God Create Other Universes?

Is there life beyond our world?

Scientists have spent hundreds of years trying to explore the far regions of space.

The Bible never mentions other universes. It only describes God creating "the heavens and the earth" and interacting with people on this planet.

This doesn't mean life can't exist on other planets. The Bible simply doesn't tell us.

It's incredible what astronomers and scientists have discovered about space.

Yet nothing is as amazing as those first words of the Bible.

> *"In the beginning, God created the heavens and the earth."*
> Genesis 1:1 (NIV).

Heart Activity

If someone you love has died, you probably feel brokenhearted.

The Bible gives a special promise for you.

> "He **heals the brokenhearted**
> and **binds up their wounds**."
> Psalm 147:3 (NIV).

God promises to comfort you and heal your broken heart.

Here is an activity for you to do as a reminder.

1. Cut out the paper heart on the next page, or draw a heart on a piece of paper.

2. On the heart, write down all of the things that are making you sad. Tear the heart into three or four pieces.

3. Find a few Band-Aids and write "God" on each one.

4. Put your broken heart back together.

Remember: God is with you and will help to heal your broken heart.

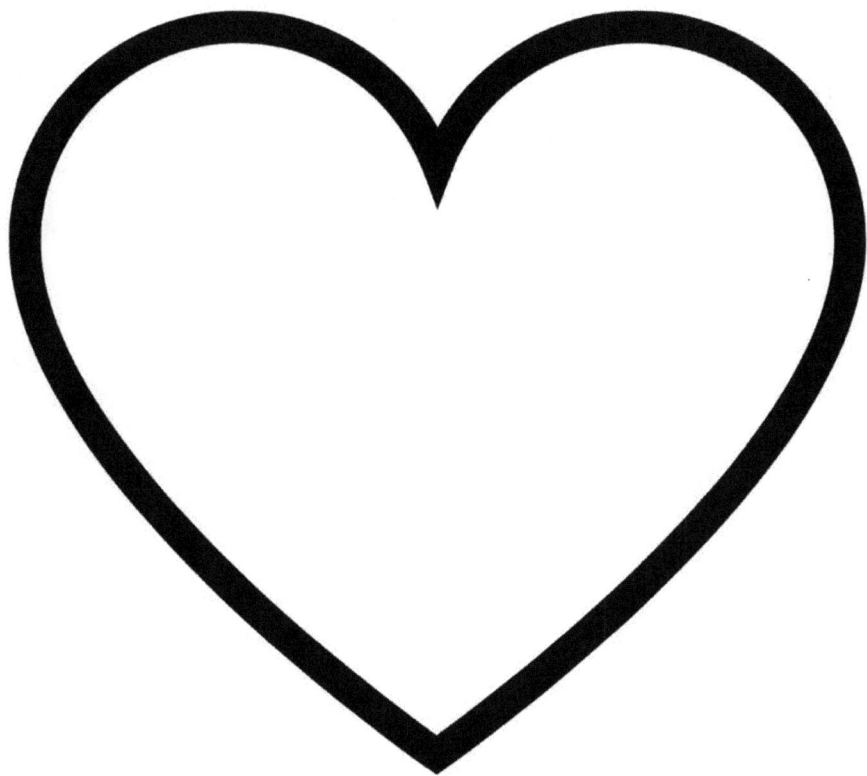

UNDERSTANDING LIFE AND DEATH

Congratulations

You have completed "UNDERSTANDING LIFE & DEATH."

Write your name and date on the certificate, and have your parent or a teacher sign it for you.

Certificate of Completion
Awarded to

_____

On _____ _____ _____
          Month   Day   Year

For completing UNDERSTANDING LIFE & DEATH

Presented by _____
                  Signature

UNDERSTANDING LIFE AND DEATH

Note To Parents

Talking about hard topics such as life and death is hard for any adult, but thinking about introducing a child to these subjects can be challenging.

Each person deals with the issue of death differently. Kids especially need space to feel things they can't verbalize or understand.

Pray that God allows you to have a sensitive spirit to see when children need additional help.

NOTE: This information is not intended to replace any advice from health or social care professionals. We suggest you consult a qualified professional if your child is struggling.

Most parents want to do the right thing. They know that it is their job to lead their children spiritually.

But so often, they are either too busy or overwhelmed.

The best thing that you can do is to be a good role model. Set an example for your children. They are always watching.

Here are some suggestions to get you started with your children.

- Make sure your children have a Bible of their own. Make sure it's age-appropriate. They can't read it if they don't understand it (see the following page recommendations).

- Provide notebooks for each child to write down what they learn. Encourage them to write down their prayer requests and the answers to their prayers.

- Encourage them to read their Bible for five minutes every day. We suggest that you begin with the book of John.

- Encourage them to write down any questions and ask you or their Sunday School teacher.

- Make time each day to read your own Bible. Kids learn by watching you. Set a good example for them to follow.

Choosing The Best Bible for Your Child

Here are some recommendations for Bibles to help your kids get excited about God's Word!

MAKE AN AGE-APPROPRIATE CHOICE.

If you want your children to enjoy reading the Bible, buy one that is easy to read, attractive, and engaging. Too often, kids struggle to look up verses at church in a Bible that has tiny print, is in a hard-to-read translation, and has no pictures or illustrations to draw them in.

Paul wrote to young Timothy,

> "And how **from childhood** you have been acquainted with the sacred writings, which are able to make you wise for salvation through faith in Christ Jesus."
> 2 Timothy 3:15 (NIV).

Timothy began studying the Bible as a young child. As parents, we want our kids to know and love God's Word, so buy them a Bible that they will understand.

BUY A BIBLE FOR EACH CHILD

Each child needs their own copy of the Bible. As parents, we spare no expense to buy our kids whatever they need to succeed in school or sports. Do the same for God's Word. Buy them a Bible that they will love to read.

The New International Version for Young Readers (NIrV), the New International Version (NIV), or the English Standard Version (ESV) are good translations for kids.

It's one of the most important investments you can make in your child's Christian education and spiritual development.

RECOMMENDED BIBLES FOR CHILDREN

Here are some examples of recommended Bibles available today.

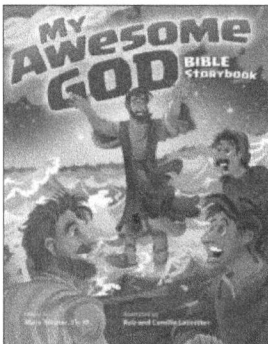

PRESCHOOL
My Awesome God Storybook

The MY AWESOME GOD Storybook Bible is ideal for parents who want to read the key stories of the Bible to their young children. This Bible includes a topical index and helpful discussion questions.

YOUNGER ELEMENTARY
NIrV Adventure Bible for Early Readers – For Ages 5–10
This is a simpler version of the children's NIV Bible created for younger readers.

One of the easiest translations is the New International Reader's Version (NIrV). The NIrV is the young reader's edition of this fun, interactive Bible that helps children learn about what they are reading through helpful information presented throughout.

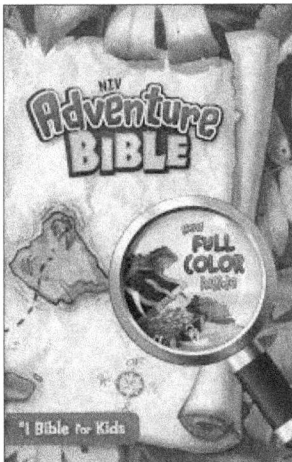

NIV Adventure Bible
For Ages 8–11
The bestselling NIV Adventure Bible® will get kids excited about reading the Scriptures! Your kids will be captivated by the full-color features that make it fun and engaging to read the Bible and memorize their favorite verses.

CSB Explorer Bible

This Bible reads similarly to the NCV translation and is filled with fun activities, maps, and images that your kids will not want to put down.

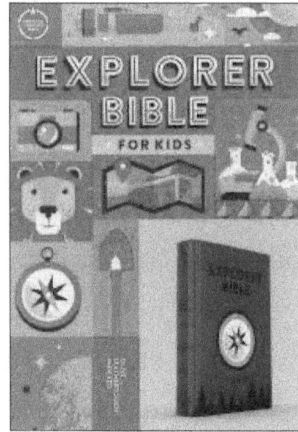

UPPER ELEMENTARY

Your preteen children can really start to master the Word of God! Here are some exciting options!

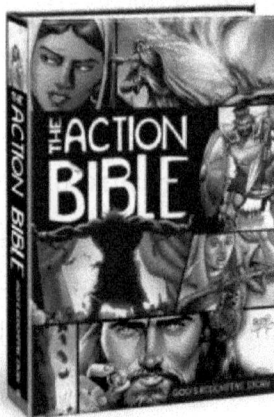

The Action Bible

The Action Bible presents the entire Bible in cool comic book illustrations. Kids will read it cover to cover many times over.

The Action Bible Study Bible

The creators of the Action Comic Bible also published a Study Bible edition in both the NIV and ESV.

The Action Study Bible is the complete text of the Bible, with select illustrations from the Action Bible throughout.

UNDERSTANDING LIFE AND DEATH

The Understanding Life Series.

UNDERSTANDING SALVATION is a short workbook designed for children ages 7-12 to use independently or with a parent.

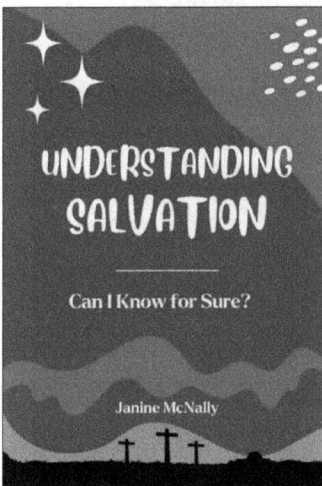

It presents the good news of Jesus in a clear and easy-to-understand way that will help them know FOR SURE that they will live with Jesus in heaven one day.

Children will learn the key principles of salvation, teaching the "Bad News" (sin) and "Good News" (Jesus), along with Bible verses and simple illustrations.

This 120-page book will help them deepen their understanding of God's grace and begin their relationship with Him.

UNDERSTANDING BAPTISM is a 95-page workbook designed for children ages 8-12 to use independently or with a parent or leader.

It is intended for those who have already expressed their belief in Jesus for salvation and have asked about being baptized.

This book answers these questions.

- How can we be saved?
- Can I be sure I am saved?
- What is baptism?
- Why should I be baptized?
- When should I be baptized?
- What happens during a baptism?

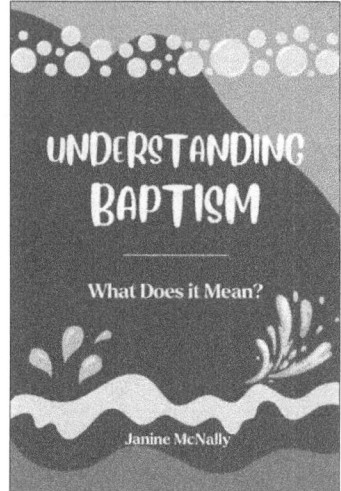

UNDERSTANDING GOD is the third book in the "Understanding Life" series for Kids, written for children ages 9-12.

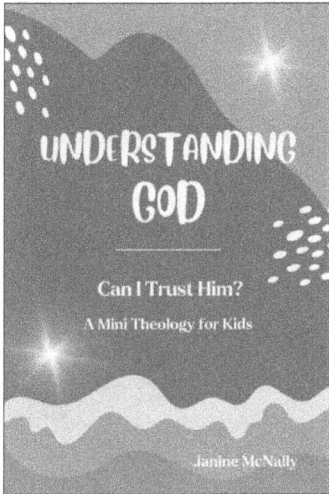

Children are asking questions every day about God, the Bible, salvation, life, death, the afterlife, angels, demons, and more.

We need to be prepared with answers, or they will look elsewhere.

This 135-page book answers the following questions.

1. What is God like?
2. How did He create the world?
3. Who Created God?
4. Who is the Holy Spirit?
5. How can Jesus be God but also be God's Son?
6. Why does God let bad things happen?
7. Can God make mistakes?
8. Does God Love Me?

This book can be used as a training resource for your volunteers or as a parent.

UNDERSTANDING the BIBLE is the fourth book in the series.

When your child asks the tough questions, do you have answers for them? Do they know how to read the Bible and apply it in their lives?

- How do we know the Bible is true?
- Is the Bible trustworthy?
- How do we know that it is really God's Word?

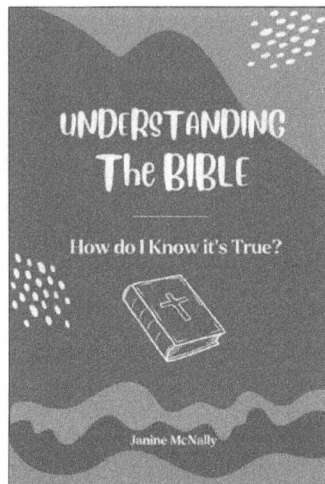

Written for children ages 8-12, this 120-page book teaches some basic Bible apologetics.

The content includes:
Three Big Words:
1. Inspiration - Written by God and Man
2. Inerrancy - No mistakes
3. Preservation

The Bible's Structure
How to Have a Quiet Time
How to Memorize God's Word

UNDERSTANDING ME addresses the big question, "Who am I?" in this 120-page book for kids ages 9-12.

Our world says, "There's no right or wrong," "We decide what is true and right," and "We can create our own identity."

At a time when kids are going through enormous changes, they are confronted with ambiguity and confusion.

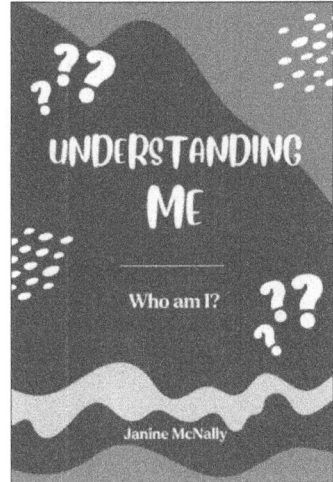

1. Who am I?
2. Am I loved?
3. Am I alone?
4. Why am I here?

Each question is handled from a Biblical perspective and ends with the hope of a new life, a new body, and a new world for those who have trusted in Jesus.

UNDERSTANDING HARD QUESTIONS is the sixth book in the "Understanding Life" series for kids.

It answers 56 of the most common questions asked by kids from a Biblical perspective and in an age-appropriate way.

- Who created God?
- Does God speak to people?
- Will God stop loving me if I keep sinning?
- How did Jesus perform miracles?
- Why do people get sick and die?
- Why did my parents get divorced?
- Can Christians lose their salvation?
- How can God forgive murderers?
- Why is sex outside of marriage wrong?
- Are there more than two genders?
- Can I be sure that I will go to heaven?

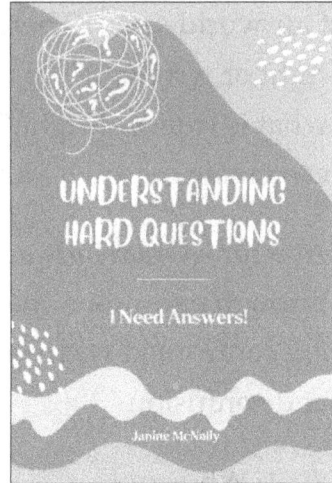

Written for kids ages 9-12, this 165-page book answers these questions using basic Bible apologetics.

UNDERSTANDING LIFE & DEATH is written for children ages 8-12 and addresses the questions that arise when a child experiences the death of a loved one.

- Why Do People Get Sick and Die?
- What Happens After You Die?
- If God Loves Me, Why Did My Dad Die?
- What is Heaven Like?
- Will Everyone Go to Heaven No Matter What They Believe?
- Do People Who Never Hear About Jesus Go to Heaven?
- Is Hell Real?
- How Could a Loving God Send People to Hell?
- Why Did God Create Satan?

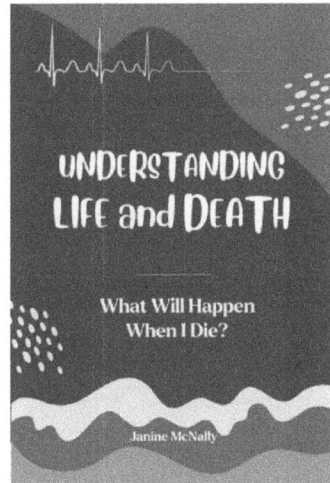

This 120-page book answers these questions and more from a Biblical perspective in an age-appropriate way. It aims to provide help and hope in times of sadness and grief.

UNDERSTANDING LIFE AND DEATH

About the Author

Originally a high school teacher in her native Australia, Janine McNally has partnered with her husband for many years of pastoral ministry.

Janine graduated with a Master of Theology from Dallas Theological Seminary and a Doctor of Ministry from Grace School of Theology.

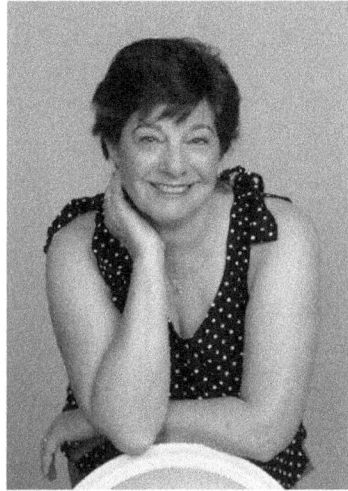

She is the author of "When You See Fireflies—Equipping Leaders and Parents to Minister Effectively to Generation Alpha," the "Understanding Life for Kids" series, seven devotional books for kids ("10 Minutes with God"), and "STEPS to Knowing Jesus" for kids and preteens.

She passionately believes in reaching kids for Jesus and enlightening leaders and parents about Generation Alpha and beyond.

Janine and Gary have been married for thirty-two years and live in Panama City, Florida.

UNDERSTANDING LIFE AND DEATH

They have three grown children, Hannah (married to Kevin), Jonathan (married to Brayton), and Jami Grace.

They also have three beautiful grandchildren, Grayson, Hunter, and Emerson.

About the Ministry

Janine McNally directs the operations of **Equipping Fireflies**, a non-profit dedicated to providing gospel-centered resources that proclaim a message that will grab the attention of this generation, break the magnetic attraction of the increasingly dark world, and lead children to the Light.

THE STORY BEHIND THE NAME

"When do we have to come inside?"
"When you see the fireflies."

Our kids loved to play outside, but as night began to fall, it was time to come in, where it was safe. Each evening, for a short time, the fireflies would light up our entire backyard. Their unmistakable glow was the signal that it was time.

Our world has become much darker. We desperately need the kids and their families to hear the call. "Come inside where it's safe." The world is rapidly becoming bleaker as the generations race by, yet our children are running towards the night.

We must proclaim a message that grabs their attention, one that they understand and that will break the magnetic attraction of the increasingly dark world.

"You are the light of the world.
Let your light shine before others that they may see your good deeds and glorify your Father in heaven."
Matthew 5:14; 16

OUR PASSION
Statistics show that most Christians trusted Christ between the ages of 3 and 12. Our passion is to reach children for Jesus and serve, equip, and encourage Children's Ministry leaders and parents.

THE GOOD NEWS
When Jesus died on the cross, He did EVERYTHING that God requires for us to go to heaven when we die."

EQUIPPING FIREFLIES

Lighting the Way for the Next Generations.
www.equippingfireflies.com

WHAT HAPPENS WHEN WE DIE?

"And these words which I command you today shall be in your heart. You shall teach them diligently to your children, and shall talk of them when you sit in your house, when you walk by the way, when you lie down, and when you rise up.
You shall bind them as a sign on your hand, and they shall be as frontlets between your eyes. You shall write them on the doorposts of your house and on your gates."
Deuteronomy 6:6-9

.